# Israel/The Reality

# Israel/The Reality

People, Places, Events
in Memorable Photographs

Edited by Cornell Capa

Preface by Nelson Glueck

Foreword by Karl Katz

Introduction by Moshe Shamir,
translated by Hillel Halkin

Consulting Editor, Micha Bar-Am

Designed by Arnold Saks

Published in association with
The Jewish Museum

The World Publishing Company
New York and Cleveland

Published by The World Publishing Company
2231 West 110th Street, Cleveland, Ohio 44102

Published simultaneously in Canada by
Nelson, Foster & Scott Ltd, and in the United
Kingdom by Thames and Hudson Ltd

First printing—1969

Library of Congress Catalog Card Number:
78-92070

Printed by Conzett and Huber, Zurich,
Switzerland

## Preface

Israel is the name of the land and its people. It spells out the story from the dawn of conscience down to this very day. "And he said, Thy name shall be called...Israel, for thou hast striven with God and men and thou hast prevailed." The designation carries with it the history of a miraculous past and the promise of peaceful creativity for the future, bound up with blessing for all peoples.

Israel is a land of sharp contrasts, of fierce light and sudden darkness, of extreme barrenness and surprising fertility, of delicate flowers and tough bushes armed with tearing spikes, of rain in scarcity and of extreme dryness over much of its expanse. It is a land of great heat by day and often bitter cold by night, of cultivable plains, high and broken plateaus, ranges of divisive hills, deep canyons and innumerable dry stream beds that on rare occasions are filled with short-lived torrents. It is distinguished by a comparatively small main river, whose significance infinitely surpasses its physical proportions. It is a strong land, where divinity once made itself apparent and where indomitable Israeli pioneers have settled and continue to strike root in ancestral soil.

The blessing and curse of the land of Israel lie in its geographical centrality. It is a crossroads on the deathless trade routes between East and West. It stands midway between Asia and Africa, between Europe and Arabia. The attempts to conquer it because of frenetic jealousies of neighboring countries or to master it as a prize or pawn in imperial ambitions and rivalries have never subsided. Hence the peaceful plowman must carry his rifle with him to the field, which should know only the rhythm of growth and the riot of verdure and flowers. Palestine, as Israel was once known from the Philistines who nearly succeeded in subduing it, has always been, as far back as it is possible to trace, a cockpit of unending conflict between mutually contending world powers. Those who survive must acquire special strengths of character and courage to live and thrive in the midst of pitiless and pathetic struggle.

Ideas, even more than men with their appetites and ambitions, have collided in the land of Israel. In this crossroads of continents and arena of empires, only the ideas of God and good as first revealed to Abraham and those who succeeded him have proved to be imperishable. The only thing of permanence that has issued from the travail of the land and of the Hebrews to whom was revealed the concept of one God, the Master of the universe and the Father of all mankind, is the increased understanding of the moral imperatives of Sacred Writ. They are indestructibly part of the total testimony of this extraordinary land.

Its character became evident when Abraham desisted from slaying his son Isaac—a revolutionary act of immense moral and religious import for all mankind. God's intervention is cited again and again in Biblical literature to emphasize the sanctity of life, the blessings of peace, the equality of human brotherhood in His eyes: "I have set before you life and death, blessing and curse; therefore choose life...." Moses climbed to the summit of God's mountain, and the Ten Commandments have been transmitted to history in his name. Amos demanded in the name of God: "Let justice roll down as waters and righteousness as a mighty stream." Isaiah, voicing God's wishes, exclaimed: "Cease to do evil, learn to do good, seek justice, relieve the oppressed, protect the fatherless, plead for the widow...." And Hillel and Jesus underscored the Levitical injunction: "Thou shalt love thy neighbor as thyself." Thus and thus only, they taught, could the love of God be expressed. This was a miraculous development of the human spirit, which is finding new strength in the modern land of Israel. The ruins of cities and villages that as a result of mankind's savagery litter the face of the earth in the form of ancient tells have been and can only continue to be counterbalanced by the pilgrim's progress, however painful and slow, in the Land of Promise and to the ends of the earth.

And nowhere has the manifestation of the divine and man's approach to it been more marked in past and present history than in the Holy Land, which I believe forms the center of the physical and spiritual heartland of the world. From that point of view, I regard Jerusalem as the world's most holy city and the Jordan as the world's most sacred stream. In the special grace that marks its uniqueness, and in the endless questing for the new dawn demanded of its peoples, I find the enduring reality of Israel.

—Nelson Glueck

## Foreword

In 1955, when I started to help plan the excavation of
an ancient site in the northern Negev, a town planner who
was with us on top of the tell on that searing day waved
his arm and pointed to a completely leveled, barren area
nearby. He said that we would get all our workmen from
the city and live in houses located between the police
station and the garage. It was a mirage!—I thought he
had sunstroke.

In 1956 we indeed had hundreds of laborers living in
attractive low-cost housing units in that city called Gath.
And our work camp was a hundred yards away from the
very businesslike police headquarters.

I have watched cities rise, universities and museums
spring into being, deserts disappear, and the land stab
into the sea. I have witnessed the character of the popu-
lation change entirely, and have lived in the land of
timeless landscapes whose Baedeker is the Bible.

It is only since 1955 that I have known Israel, and I had
always hoped that the things I experienced were being
properly recorded by photographers. Happily, they were.
In fact, over a period beginning long before my recent
arrival, they provided the subject for the sensitive eyes
and lenses of many fine photographers, who had come to
this country to document its landscape, its people, and
its history.

When I assumed the directorship of The Jewish Museum
in New York I wanted to show there the excitement I had
felt watching Israel change under my very eyes. I knew
that photography was the medium that would best capture
and communicate this. I also knew that the well-known
photojournalist Cornell Capa had much knowledge of
and interest in Israel. I respected his judgment and asked
him to direct an exhibition on the subject. After intensive
research, he decided on a new and unusual approach
to a thematic exhibition: a division of most of the works
into distinct, self contained photo-essays by individual
photographers, both Israeli and foreign, each one in time
and spirit presenting the essence of one aspect of the
subject. In many instances Capa discovered both early
photographs and works by contemporary photographers
that had never been shown publicly. The individual
essays together with general collections on specific

themes and events capture, in the exhibition and in this book developed from it, a multifaceted view of the ancient/new country.

Moshe Shamir's text corresponds, in a sense, to the photographers' essays, and complements them. It, too, is composed of images seen and remembered, fleeting moments captured by a swift, keen eye, and translated into words.

—Karl Katz

## Acknowledgments

Our thanks and appreciation are due to the following persons and organizations for their kind and valued cooperation, particularly in the acquisition of photographs: Shlomo Shva, who acted as consultant on historical photographs; David Eldan of the Israel Government Press Office; Adina Haran and the Central Zionist Archives, Jerusalem, for works by Ben-Dov, Zvi Oron and other historical photographers; Anina Kaplan and the Museum of History of Tel Aviv for photographs by Abraham Soskin; Dov Amitai and the Photographers Guild of Kibbutz Haarzi; Peter Merom of the Israel Photo Annual; Lillie Schultz of the Weizmann Institute; Sara Yodfat and Miss Michal of Keren Hayesod (the United Israel Appeal Photo Archives, Jerusalem) for photographs on immigration; and Mr. Kopilov of the Hagana Archives, and Miss Dinaburg of the Labor Archive, both in Tel Aviv.

We would like to extend our thanks as well to Ralph Baum, Igor Bakht, Eliashiv Ben Horin, Peter Brunswick, Rabbi Herbert Friedman, Edward Ginsberg, Pamela Ilott, Amit Kali, Alexander Kaufman, Marjorie Morris, Ralph Steiner, Danielle Wexler, and Amram Zur for their kind and generous support.

This publication has been made possible through a grant from EL AL Israel Airlines.

## Introduction

Ringo is the first to leap from the car. He charges with a bark down the sandy slope, stopping only when a foamy wave washes over his feet and sends him back in full retreat. My son jumps out after him but pauses halfway at the first curious shell or piece of driftwood covered with seaweed. After locking the car I follow them slowly toward the shore, my feet chafing against the sand, which has been packed hard by last night's storm and coated with a thin layer of salt. We like our seashore on gray, wintry mornings like these. We like to look for what the waves have left behind.

For me it is a love that goes back to my childhood. We lived in a small house on the beach. On the near horizon, south of our small white city, was Jaffa's familiar dark silhouette: the gradual rise toward the west, the high exclamation point of the minaret, and then the quick drop down to the harbor and the water. The nicest things came from the harbor. It was then the country's main port, though it did not have a single wharf. The ships dropped anchor far beyond the breakers, where they waited for the oared dinghies to bring them out crates of oranges. In the winter there were storms in which the dinghies would sometimes capsize, and the waves carried the crates to the foot of the casino, from where we dragged them homeward through the sand.

Sometimes there were rotten apples or bolts of fabric. Once a broken oar. Another time a bloated cat, full of water and death. The waves were followed by the wind, which swept clean the sand and the litter left by summer. Here I once came across the greatest find of all my young days: a real, shiny shilling.

During one of the worst of these storms the waves washed a whole ship ashore. She was the *Bayern,* out of Germany, a big handsome vessel wedged between the rocks. On Saturday the entire town turned out to have a look at her from up close, to wave at the sailors and argue about how far she was from shore. Alert Arab vendors came along, with pretzels and bright paper whirligigs furiously spinning in the strong sea breeze. When the ship remained stuck, people began to come from all over— from Jerusalem, from the mountains. That winter we had a regular carnival on the sandy shore.

My son is shouting at me in the distance, waving his arms excitedly. I am not walking fast enough; he wants me to run. There is a round metal object stuck in the sand with something that looks like an electric wire protruding from one side. Danger: it could be a mine. In school they have been told not to touch. What on earth is a bicycle head-light doing here?

We climb up a steep limestone hill. This rough, crumbly, treacherous rock is entirely the product of the waves. They built it, they shaped it, and now they are dissolving and destroying it. There are hardly any tides along our coast, but the waves refuse to give it any peace. It is as though the stubborn old Mediterranean were still unhappy with the shape of our land, and goes right on modeling it, adding here, subtracting there.

So much for geography. We are shaped by the waves of history too.

Once my boy returned from school on the eve of a Jewish holiday grumbling, "I'm tired of hearing about these holidays all the time." "Why? What's the matter?" "It's always the same story. Either they killed the Jews or else they wanted to kill them. On Succoth they were in the desert because the Egyptians wanted to kill them, and on Hanukkah the Greeks killed them, and on the Eleventh of Adar the Arabs killed Trumpeldor and burned Tel-Hai, and on Purim Haman wanted to kill them, and on Passover Pharaoh ordered the babies to be drowned, and on Lag b'Omer the Romans killed whoever was studying the Torah. I don't get it. What is it with these holidays of ours?"

Our beach bears the name of our neighborhood. The neighborhood bears the name of a Jew from Bulgaria. He was the leader of the people who built their houses here —a small piece of Bulgarian life that the waves washed ashore. The grandmothers still speak the Ladino that their forebears had brought from medieval Spain, and when the watermelon vendor stops his wagon beneath your window every morning, you can hear the proud Castilian timbre of their voices from one end of the street to the other. The soft-spoken grocer writes down your purchases in Bulgarian, in Slavic letters. His speech has a pleasant, intimate, Russian-sounding ring. The younger generation speaks Hebrew. It is a peaceful neighborhood of hard-working people: little white houses, straight streets shaded by pines. In the courtyards are fruit trees, gardens, and flowers.

Each morning the neighborhood empties of its men and children. it is the liveliest, noisiest time of day. A hundred new beginnings collide and rub shoulders on the one main street. The children who go to the local school are of course the most colorful, the most animated, the loudest of all. But just as amusing is the bank clerk running to catch the bus as though his life depended on it, his attaché case flailing in one hand. Soldiers of both sexes who grew up here wait to thumb a ride back to their bases with an utterly patronizing air. Finished with his daily run, the milkman sits rocking among empty bottles in his cart and refuses to prod his unassuming donkey, though the bus behind him is forced to slow to a crawl until the next stop.

Cleaning women get off. The bank clerk is there in time, but a crowd of high-school students have beaten him to it. The bus is always packed at this hour. The nimblest of the students fights his way to the last empty seat and sits with his briefcase on his knees. Soon a friend has added his briefcase, and then comes another, until there is a swaying column of them.

A lonely old woman remains behind in the empty street. She will walk with measured steps as far as the corner, stop, look around. She will go no further until someone shows her the way to the cemetery.

Our bus line runs to Tel Aviv's new cemetery. You can always tell the ones who are going there—the unshaven men in old hats, the women in sunglasses and kerchiefs. Amid the bright, noisy stream flows this quiet current. On the Day of Memorial for the Holocaust, or the Day of Memorial for Israel's fallen soldiers, they fill every seat on the bus. Then it is as though the shadow of a funeral has passed through all the streets until reaching ours, which is bounded at one end by the waves and at the other by tombstones.

But the real life of the neighborhood goes on in its side streets. Here are the grocery stores, the newspaper stands, the local movie house, the pharmacy. The fat, fatherly druggist is also the neighborhood physician. You come and tell him what ails you, and he prescribes a remedy. It is a pharmacy of the old type: a wide room, plain wooden chairs along the wall, a long counter covered with bottles and vials and glass jars full of honey candy that sells by the gram and is wrapped in old newspapers. Incidentally, this is the only pharmacy in Israel where you can buy mineral water from the Bulgarian spas. And the old folk, all the old folk of the neighborhood, assemble here. They come every morning to sit down in the chairs by the wall, and slump silently for hours on end. There is no safer place than a pharmacy.

"The living corpse" is always the last to arrive. He brings his own chair, or, rather, his chair brings him. It is not a wheelchair, but an ordinary house chair. He steps out into the street pushing it ahead of him. After a few steps he halts, shuffles forward, and sits down in the middle of the street. Then he gets up, pushes it forward a few more steps, stops, and sits again. At approximately ten o'clock he reaches the pharmacy. Everyone knows there is no need to help him. Not until he has sat one last time right by the door does he push his chair inside, up against the wall, and take a seat among his companions.

They are good to have around, the old folk, because the druggist has a passion for dominos, and next door to the pharmacy is a cafe. A Bulgarian cafe is like a Turkish cafe and a Turkish cafe is like an Arab cafe: tables, dominos, and little cups of black coffee. Later in the afternoon the tables are all taken, and the air is filled with the click-clack of the tiles. Then the druggist deserts his post and steals off to stand behind the players and watch the game, his big, paunchy body still in its white smock. If someone stops at the pharmacy to ask for him, the old folk will know where he is.

It was like that the time they brought in the injured plasterer. On the street stood the contractor's pickup truck, both cab doors open wide. A little man was shouting inside, his upraised hands bleeding over his bare arms, which were encrusted with dirty splotches of plaster and lime. The druggist told the contractor to make him sit down and hurried to the shelves behind the counter. But the plasterer kept shouting all the while the druggist was cleaning his wounds. It was all the contractor's fault. "Over my dead body that goddamned glazier is going to put in his goddamned windows before I finish plastering! And don't tell me it can be done at the same time. I know my job. I'll break every one of his windows, and then I'll go on to his head! First I finish plastering and then you can do with the house what you want—you can burn the damn thing if you like. How can I work when he's running around with his windows? And don't give me any of your crap about the division of labor. You, what do you know about labor? Go on, go on, get out of here—go tell him you're taking out the windows because I'm going back there and break every one of them, do you hear me?"

The old folk sat along the wall and murmured in Bulgarian, "The whole neighborhood's going to the dogs...."


To the south, cityward, the neighborhoods of the rich keep creeping up on us, dragging along their wide roads and their columns of telephone poles and high-tension wires. Suddenly, all at once, they are upon us.

If anything in this country looks as though the waves have washed it ashore overnight, it is one of these clusters of new buildings. Sand dunes everywhere, here and there a splotch of sparse vegetation, a single road that comes and goes again, and suddenly, in the midst of it all, there it stands with straight, vertical lines and proud, cold cleanliness—eight stories, ten stories, fourteen stories. The poets used to write that Tel Aviv was a child of the dunes. That was in the city's first years, when it still conformed to the natural contours of the land. The houses went up by the sycamore trees and on the slopes of the vineyards; the streets were laid over the old camel and goat paths. There are still a few old streets in Tel Aviv that can be said to loop or climb or plunge sharply to the sea. But these years of innocence are gone forever; now everything is leveled before the buildings go up.

Take the square kilometer between us and the city: half of it already urban, the other half still open country. And just as the city creeps up on the country, so the country creeps back into the city. The most brazen of the infiltrators are the watermelon vendors. They take their place by the main highway and do not care that the gas station has already opened a Wimpy's, or that the cars get larger and faster all the time, or that the 'country club' has closed off a wide area with a high fence. They pay no attention to the giant gas tanks proliferating on one side and the smoke-stacks of the electric company rising ever higher on the other. They take their place by the highway and in no time convert it into home.

They return here year after year in the middle of the summer to build wooden booths covered with burlap on the shoulder of the road. They fill them with green piles of watermelons, bring their wives and children, and sleep on a rickety bed or on the sand, lighting up the night with a smoky field lantern. There they wait with confident patience for the cars to pull up and for their passengers to step out and pick a melon, squeeze it and listen to its sweet inner juices, put their faith in the rusty scales and stone weights, haggle over the price, and pay for it in the end with good, crisp money.

Some of these melons grow where we live, next to the green peppers, the tomatoes, the lettuce, and the egg-plant. At the same hour of the morning when the neighbor-hood empties of its men and children, in rumble the trucks with signs that say 'Passengers' and three rows of benches in the back, bringing field hands from the Arab villages near the border. In each the radio blasts a musi-cal program from Cairo, to which the women sing and clap hands. They all pile out at the end of the street, which looks for a moment like an exotic marketplace. But the driver, who is also the straw boss, has already turned off the radio and taken command. The women are sent by groups to the vegetable patches that stretch out in every direction, and soon the fields are dotted with bright daubs of undulating color.

I chanced upon some of them late one afternoon as I was coming home. They were sitting and chatting quietly in a long line, pink by green by yellow by blue, enjoying a brief rest in the shade before the truck came to pick them up. Next to one lay a pile of branches and broken boards which she had managed to gather in empty lots. Another had a large cardboard box with smaller boxes inside it. Further on another bundle of firewood, and a plain sheet of tin which could serve to cover a stove or a chicken coop.

It made me quietly happy to see them leaning against the stone fence around my courtyard, shielded by the pleasant coolness of my trees. It was as if my house had guests.

But they fell silent as I passed. I didn't say a word and neither did they. They were the Arabs. I was the Jews.

I remember an Arab who was searching for a human glance in Dizengoff Circle in Tel Aviv. There is no place in Israel where so many people can be found together at four o'clock in the afternoon. He was dressed in a peasant robe and wore a *kaffia* on his head. His bare feet were wedged into a pair of new shoes. One might have thought he was simply out for a stroll were not his movements so confused. He wandered through the circular plaza, around which roared a steady stream of vehicles, stopping now and then as though he had remembered something and then drifting onward with small, hesitant steps. He was bewildered, lost, truly miserable.

I thought of going over to say a friendly word or to offer my assistance, but just then a change came over him. He had seen something. For a moment he stood still, his gaze riveted upon whatever it was beyond the circle, and then set out with a purposeful stride. He passed among the promenaders, reached the street, descended into the sluggish flow of traffic and crossed to the opposite corner. I followed him.

A crowd of women surrounded the cart of an apricot vendor. He was crying his wares at the top of his voice while weighing out bags filled with fruit, bargaining with the housewives, and keeping a sharp eye on their even sharper hands. The Arab halted outside the commotion and took two small steps toward the horse harnessed to the cart. When he had sidled up to it, he raised his hand and stroked it on its back. From there the hand moved up the neck and over the top of the head, then glided slowly down to the nose. The horse's soft lips trembled. He pricked up his ears and turned to look at the man standing beside him.

North of Dizengoff Circle stretches the liveliest, most crowded, and most expensive kilometer in the whole state of Israel. In the middle of it, by a sidewalk table, a poet once sat and waited for twenty years. He came every evening right after sunset, when the tables were still empty, and could be seen sitting by himself long after midnight, when the tables were empty again. The cafe grew up around him, changed its decor and its customers, but still he sat at the same table with an intense look on his face, his jaw tilted forward, his legs crossed, always a long cigarette-holder and a pack of cheap cigarettes by a half-drunk cup of tea.

He always sat by himself, conspicuous because of his high forehead, his great shock of hair, his long, carefully groomed sideburns—conspicuous too because of his loneliness amid the convivial crowd. Twenty years.... Now his table is always full, of friends, of disciples, of admirers. They all have long hair and carefully groomed sideburns. Some of them even understand his poems, sometimes.

The twenty poems he wrote in the course of these twenty years comprise a wonderful, personal, and inaccessible world. It is a private ghetto in which only one person lives. All this person's possessions have come from afar, with the waves. His verses know nothing of grammar—they are simply washed up on the shores of his pages. Three languages have left their pebbles there or their cold sea monsters; the half-remembered hours of childhood have deposited a smell of disintegrating flotsam. Perhaps two words and three images of all that accidentally passed and grew weary by his table during those twenty years in the cafe are also there. A Bedouin from the Negev becomes a Jewish Hassid from a Polish village; Arabic words with Yiddish intonations are joined together in Hebrew sentences like broken shells whose missing halves will never be found.

He has written a small cycle of poems consisting of letters that were written to him, lost, and then rewritten by him: letters from his mother, his father, his brother, his sister—delivered and lost. Father, mother, brother, and sister, he tells you, were lost without being delivered, and he turns the pack of cigarettes over and over, as if somewhere it had a right side, and one must find it and not give up.

"It's ludicrous," he says, "this idealization of what's here and now. As if here we were born—this moment—in good health. The good earth. Geography for beginners. Hebrew for beginners. History for beginners."

"Whenever there's a storm," I said, "I myself would like to be a wave."

"Waves are a product too," he answered, "and a rather boring one."

"Give me two thousand years of boredom," I said. "Then we can discuss it."

He thinks that whoever has no piece of the ghetto in him is not a Jew. And a Jew who is not a Jew is not a man. This is why he does not like anything to be clean, complete, correct. "This ideal of the Sabra, of the new, free Jew in his new homeland. New from what? Free from what? If you were to confront your nonchalant Sabra with the frightened Jew of the ghetto, yes, your permanently frightened Jew—then the Sabra becomes your bully of a gentile. Your Sabra is the real goy."

My Sabra. Perhaps he is the kibbutznik, not yet three years old, who spends the night on a field cot in a shelter next to another boy two months younger than himself. Outside thunders a winter storm, the lightning flashing through the chinks of the door. "Don't be afraid, Dani," he comforts his wailing friend. "Just make believe we're being shelled."

In the Sinai Peninsula it rains two days a year. On one of these days we were traveling in a convoy of jeeps from the mountainous region around Mount Sinai and the Monastery of Saint Catherine to the coastal strip across from Suez and the Egyptian lines. The evening descended quickly, and we sat with weapons ready beneath our sleeveless army ponchos. In these parts it is best not to take chances. Which is perhaps why the jeep stopped so sharply: under the glare of its headlights one of the rocks by the roadside had risen to become a man, a young Israeli. He approached us wrapped in a dripping blanket. We had already begun to move over and make room when we discovered that he was heading in the other direction, back to the monastery. Had he taken leave of his senses? The nearest human habitation was more than a two hours' drive across fifty kilometers of wadi and desert. We suggested he come with us and try again the next day. Nothing doing. He had his C-rations. He had his gun. He had shelter among the rocks. Something was bound to come in his direction sooner or later. And if not, the rain would stop, and he could always hike it. What were fifty kilometers, after all? A day's walk.

I'll never forget that Sabra, the man in the blanket, lit up in flashes by our rear lights and finally disappearing from sight to turn back into a stone by the roadside.

Last winter's storms washed a strange and terrible object ashore near Gaza, and the Arab fisherman who found it hurried to inform the Israeli police post. It was a float which had come loose from an Israeli submarine that had vanished mysteriously a year before on a homeward voyage. Twenty-seven years previously, during the grimmest days of World War II, one of the first Palmach units set out in a PT boat on a sabotage mission for the British army. The target was a military installation in Lebanon that was being used at the time to assist the German war effort. They never reached it, and they never came back. Twenty-three of them. The number of men on the sunken submarine was exactly three times as many. On the bottom of the Mediterranean the Sabras hold a majority.

The Sabras are a small minority in the Knesset, in the government, in the philharmonic orchestra. They are represented somewhat better in the theater and in literature. Among Israel's upper classes, its property owners, they are a decided minority. Their position is improving among professors and scientists, and among the fliers in the air force they form a majority of nearly one hundred percent. In the discotheques too. And among the tractor drivers, which makes them a majority of those who rise early all over Israel.

The tractor drivers have always been early risers. The first shift begins at four a.m., and during the autumn sowing season the nights are already cold. So they hurry to the communal kitchen to gulp something hot, and pick up the lunchboxes and thermoses that are waiting for them. Then they make their way into the darkness. A cold east wind carries the redolence of far fields, and there is no way of knowing whether the humming in the air comes from the stars or from one's own sleep-sodden head. They awaken together with their tractors: the steel beasts let out a roar and the night is over. By the time they are out on the dark trails, their headlights groping ahead of them, only a thin strip of the pale new day is showing in the east.

Today many kibbutzim have a tractor that is up and about even earlier: the sweeper-tractor. It noses over the roads among the fields with a mine detector attached to its front end, combing the paths between the banana groves, skirting the fish ponds, checking them out for the workers, the wagons, the tractors to come. By sunrise they will all be on the job. Except for the children, who sleep later in shelters below ground.

In Jerusalem too, in early autumn, men rise early for the penitential prayers that precede the Days of Awe. I used to lie with my eyes wide open and listen to the soft voice of the night crier as he approached from beyond the narrow lanes and the stone walls, to his monotonous call that seemed to melt back into the darkness: *"Selihot…selihot…."*
It was not hard to figure out his route. After leaving his house near the synagogue, he walked down the narrow street that led to the main avenue. But there was little for him to do there, because there were only stores and homes that belonged to another synagogue. Retracing his steps, he cut through the small wood by the school and entered the heart of our quarter, passing under the windows along one side of the street and then back under the windows on the other. Then he began to draw nearer to our house, climbing slowly up the winding street, sounding his mild summons to prayer at equally spaced intervals. As he approached, one could count the number of steps that he took between one call and the next. The silent stone houses awakened; an iron door creaked open and slammed shut. I would lie there in the darkness listening to the street fill with hurrying footsteps. The crier's voice had already faded into the distance, but outside there was a sudden burst of life. Then that too died down. Once again there was silence.

When gayety comes, however, it falls upon the quarter like a conflagration. The street begins to run, children shout to one another, housewives strip off their aprons and patter down the sidewalks in their sandals. Only then do you first hear the sound of the celebration itself, like an approaching torrent.

From up close it may look like some terrible disaster. A dark crowd of men crushed together, for example, pushing in toward the center, swaying slowly back and forth, while over their heads rises a steady clamor. Not until the jam suddenly parts before your eyes do you see the shrouded scroll in the middle, one man with his eyes shut hugging it to his breast, while the young yeshivah students dance around in a circle, thrusting their beards up toward the sky, clapping their hands, and singing a single melody that surges and sinks and rises again without cease.

A new Torah is being brought to the synagogue.

Another crowd in black once stood on the seashore and tendered a whispered prayer. Jews had come for *tashlich* at the close of Rosh Hashanah to purge their pockets, their bodies, and their hearts of the past year's sins. It was an overcast evening. The waves were slow and foamless but very heavy. I remember it all very well. I was a boy at the time and I liked to go down to the sea. Suddenly a dinghy appeared among the waves, hurtling in very quickly. The people on shore retreated in fright. Two young men in bathing suits jumped from the boat, grabbed it by its sides, and steered it toward the beach. With the help of a wave they managed to drag it up on the hard sand. Only then did they notice the crowd that stood there and stared at them —the old men, the old women, the children in skullcaps, the solemn, dignified Jews in dark clothes with little books in their hands. For a second the two men looked like burglars trapped by a sudden spotlight. Naked and smooth-skinned, they stood on each side of the boat looking silently at the bewildered, heavily attired crowd. But it was the crowd that gave way. The old men backed off, pulling along the children, who kept looking back.

The two men jumped back into the boat and began to throw out metal parts, a wooden door, crates, a long iron chain. I knew where the loot came from. One could see it despite the thick fog—the illegal immigrant ship wrecked on the rocks. It had arrived one night over a year before and had run aground near shore while trying to elude the British. Its passengers vanished the same night into nearby houses. They were given hot tea to drink and fresh clothes to wear, and were hidden for months. The ship itself remained stranded for years. For a long while scavengers stripped it of whatever they could, and little by little the great corpse was picked clean. Time and the waves did the rest.

Today most immigrants come by air. Sometimes a special flight arrives containing immigrants only, and it circles a few minutes to show them the country from above. It does not take long to show so small a land: a white strip of coast, a band of reddish lowlands, a gray mountain range, golden-brown desert spaces. And everywhere is the never-ending war of live, effervescent green against dead, dry yellow.

Better to stand on the ground with one's shoes off. Why are only bare feet permitted to touch holy soil? What kind of country have they been brought to? It will take time. I ask myself: can you make anyone *see* a country? Better perhaps to shut one's eyes and listen to it, smell it, feel it.

I can hear the muted whisper of the pine needles in the little forest near Jerusalem. Even on the most scorching summer day there is always an afternoon breeze in the hills. You sit under the trees with the wind brushing the sweat from your face (careful you do not lean against the bark—the sap sticks to your hair, your shirt—you will never get rid of it!), the distances blurred by the heat waves. The ground at your feet is carpeted by pine needles, littered with small mementos of the past: a rusty can, a rifle cartridge, two stones painted white, the smoke-corroded hollow of a rock. The thin, translucent shadows of the trees tremble above like a man caressing his memories.

In the citrus groves in the lowlands the shade is steady and thick. I used to like to lie by myself in the shade of the old lemon trees. I'd have to crawl on all fours under the branches bowed beneath their load of fruit. Within was a world of eternal half-light. The earth was soft and warm, and the dry leaves crackled and crumbled when you touched them. Next your hand began to grope for one of the pendulous lemons. It wasn't easily picked but the struggle was pleasant: The roughness of the rind, the frightened lizard that sent a rustle up the trunk, and the smell—yes, the smell most of all—the quick, sharp, stinging aroma of the plucked green leaf and the bitten fruit.

And how to describe the scent of mint in the brush of the wadis? It was not shut up within itself like the fragrance of the lemons. It filled the whole gully, as if announcing from afar: water. But you did not always find water, especially not toward the end of summer. We used to pick the fleshy, hairy leaves and roll them between our fingers until their pungency gave us the strength to drag our heavy packs and swollen feet to the next ravine and the next hope. Even when we did find water it was never drinkable. But you could take off your shoes and dip your feet in the slippery-smooth slime over which clear-winged dragonflies skated on air. The feel of the thick mud as it slid its soft tongues between your toes tempted you to plunge in deeper and deeper until finally you couldn't resist wading right through the stagnant water, your cautious soles fondling their way across the bottom.

The feel of a foot on the hot, dry earth of a plowed field. The children of these immigrants will get to know the land first with their bare feet. They will learn the names of the soils with their soles. They will study the clods in the fields of heavy clay, the fat lumps of earth that struggle to stay to-gether, and they will be able to call out the color with their eyes shut: dark chocolate, almost black—a black that gleams as though polished by the turning plow blade. And they will learn to tell these from the clumps of yellow to reddish-brown orchard loam that turn to dust upon con-tact. They will learn the feel of the hill soil with its comple-ment of tiny pebbles, and of the powdery loess of the Negev which turns dark in the rain but is as white as flour in the summer when the sandstorms blow and cover every unconcealed inch of your body with it. They will come to know the pure sand of the seashore, hard and shiny like pavement by the water but warm and soft on the white dunes. They will learn to watch out on the shores of Eilat, which bristle all over with bits of coral and shell and the remains of strange creatures from tropical seas. They will watch out, but they will walk on them anyway, barefoot.

At noon the sun will be over the sea and an incandescent strip of water will extend like a blinding river from infinity to the spot where the small boy stands shading his eyes. When I was that boy I used to think that one day a ship of gold would sail down this river bringing the Messiah.

My son does not have the patience to wait. Last autumn we took a trip to Eilat with several other families. We staked out a section of beach, pitched our tents, put on our bath-ing suits, and sent the children off for a swim. We were camped not far from the border, and the distance from our tents to the houses in Jordanian Aqaba was about the same as the distance to downtown Eilat. In fact, that is why we had chosen the place, which was so terribly peaceful precisely because most people liked to avoid it.

On our way down to Eilat, flying along the broad new Arava highway, we had seen an unusual military display: a smoke grenade, a helicopter touching down, jeeps in battle formation. That evening we heard the news on the radio. A mine, one dead, another "incident." But we were not going to let it spoil our plans: three days of games and campfires and swimming and shell-gathering in the sun. To forget. To surrender to the purposeless rhythms of life's elementary functions. To let the soup boiling on the stove be the center of all existence. And the children, we were sure, were immersed in a paradise of their own.

Early on the first morning the children disappeared. They returned when the coffee was on the fire, whispering among themselves. We could not interest them in any of our projects. First they had something terribly important (and terribly secret!) of their own to arrange. My son went to look for a piece of paper, a big white piece. His next request was for a pencil or crayon. Why? He would not say.

As the day progressed, and hour followed hour along that marvelous coast, the whole thing slipped from our minds. The children kept distracting us with all kinds of curious questions. Which way did the current flow along the shore? How did the wind blow by night and how did it blow by day? Did anyone know how far it was to Aqaba? Were there a lot of Jordanian soldiers there?

Only at nightfall, his head peeping out of his sleeping bag in the seclusion of our tent, could my son control himself no longer:

"Daddy...do you know what we did today? We made paper boats. Two of them. And we put them way out on the water so they'd sail. But first we wrote on them why don't they make peace with us. Dear Soldiers of the Arab Legion, Aqaba, Jordan, why don't you make peace with us? Signed, a boy and a girl from Israel. Whoever finds this letter please give it to the Arab Legion, Aqaba, Jordan...."

The waves have not washed it up yet.

—Moshe Shamir. Translated by Hillel Halkin

# The Photographers

**Shlomo Arad**
Born Poland, emigrated to Israel 1947. News photographer. Lives in Tel Aviv.

**Mordo Avrahamov**
Born Bulgaria, emigrated to Israel 1939. Professional gardener. Lives in Kibbutz Yakum.

**Micha Bar-Am**
Born Germany, emigrated to Israel 1936. Magazine photographer. Author of two books. Has photographed Israel's army since his own Palmach days. One of team covering Eichmann trial. Lives in Tel Aviv.

**Yaakov Ben-Dov**
Born Russia, emigrated to Israel 1908. Recorded Israel under British Mandate and after. Active in public service. Died 1968.

**Werner Braun**
Born Germany, emigrated to Israel 1936. Free-lance photographer. Especially interested in aerial and underwater photography. One of team covering Eichmann trial. Lives in Jerusalem.

**Cornell Capa**
American, born Hungary. Magazine photographer. Author of several books; creator of many exhibitions. Visited Israel 1967, covering war and aftermath. Lives in New York.

**Robert Capa**
American, born Hungary. Legendary chronicler of war, starting in Spain 1936. Recorded birth struggles of Israel on numerous visits 1948-1952. Killed Indo-China 1954.

**Boris Carmi**
Born Russia, emigrated to Israel 1939. News photographer since participation in War of Liberation. Author of several books. Lives in Tel Aviv.

**Richard Latimer Cleave**
Born England. Physician turned photographer. Author of book on Crusader Castles. Now specializes in audio-visual lectures on the Near East. Lives in Jerusalem.

**Fritz Cohn**
Born Germany, emigrated to Israel 1937. Official government press photographer. One of team covering the Eichmann trial. Lives in Tel Aviv.

**Amiram Erev**
Born Israel. For past twenty years official photographer of Solel Boneh, Israeli building cooperative. Lives in Kiryat Tivon.

**Peter Fink**
Born United States. Free-lance photographer. Author of a book; has appeared in many exhibitions. Has visited Israel three times since 1960. Lives in New York.

**Leonard Freed**
Born United States. Free-lance photographer. Especially interested in minority groups; author of books on Jews in Amsterdam and in Germany, and on Negroes in United States. Visited Israel following Six Day War 1967, remained through 1968. Lives in New York.

**Burt Glinn**
Born United States. Magazine photographer. Noted for *Holiday* travel essays; author of books on Soviet Union and Japan. Has visited Israel several times. Lives in New York.

**Paul Gross**
Born Rumania, emigrated to Israel 1947. Free-lance photographer. Especially interested in aspects of everyday life. Lives in Tel Aviv.

**Charles Harbutt**
Born United States. Magazine photographer. Spent several months in Israel and Jordan as "pilgrim with a camera" 1966-1967, including period of Six Day War. Lives in New York.

**David Harris**
Born Israel. Free-lance photographer. Known especially for coverage of archaeology. Lives in Jerusalem.

**Erich Hartmann**
American, born Germany. Magazine photographer. Has appeared in several exhibitions. Has visited Israel several times. Lives in New York.

**Ken Heyman**
Born United States. Noted for books, magazine essays, exhibitions. Visited Israel 1965. Lives in New York.

**Efrem Ilani**
Born Germany, emigrated to Israel 1934. Free-lance photographer. Lives in Jerusalem.

**Izis (Israel Bidermanas)**
French, born Lithuania. Free-lance photographer. Author of many books; has appeared in several exhibitions. Visited Israel 1952. Lives in Paris.

**Simpson Kalisher**
Born United States. Magazine photographer. Has appeared in several exhibitions. Visited Israel 1962. Lives in New York.

**Leo Kann**
Born Austria. Traveled to Israel 1910-1911. Upon return to Vienna 1912, published 400 pictures.

**Rolf Michael Kneller**
Born Germany, emigrated to Israel 1939. Film-maker and free-lance photographer. Especially interested in portraits. Lives in Jerusalem.

**Moshe Lapidot**
Born Israel. Professional locksmith. Especially interested in documenting childhood and growth of the Sabra generation. Lives in Kibbutz Mirza.

**Archie Lieberman**
Born United States. Magazine photographer. Author of several books, including *The Israelis 1965*. Lives in Chicago.

**David Maestro**
Born Yugoslavia, emigrated to Israel 1940. Photographer, painter, and teacher. Lives in Haifa.

**Donald McCullin**
Born England. News and magazine photographer. Noted for war pictures. Covered battle for Jerusalem 1967. Lives in London.

**Peter Merom**
Born Germany, emigrated to Israel 1934. Photographer and editor. Has produced more than twenty books; has appeared in several exhibitions. Editor of Israel Photo Annual. Lives in Kibbutz Hulata.

**Arnold Newman**
Born United States. Magazine photographer. Noted for portraits; has appeared in many exhibitions. Acting curator of photographic collection, Israel Museum in Jerusalem. Frequent visitor to Israel. Lives in New York.

**Zvi Oron**
Born Poland, educated Russia. Served in Jewish Legion against Turks, World War I; then settled in Tel Aviv. Photographed Mandate period 1920-1948. Lives in Ashdod.

**Yitzhak Ostrovsky**
Born Israel. News and magazine photographer. Lives in Tel Aviv.

**David Perlmutter**
Born Poland, emigrated to Israel 1940. Free-lance photographer. Has had work in several books and exhibitions. Lives in Kibbutz Emek-Sorek.

**Gideon Raz**
Born Israel. Free-lance photographer and professional machinist. Has appeared in several exhibitions. Lives in Kibbutz Shuval.

**David Rubinger**
Born Austria, emigrated to Israel 1939. Magazine photographer. Has documented Israel's history since 1946. Lives in Jerusalem.

**Paul Schutzer**
Born United States. Staff photographer for *Life*. Frequent visitor to Israel from war of 1956. Killed near Gaza June 5, 1967.

**David Seymour ("Chim")**
Born Poland, emigrated to France 1933, and to United States 1939. Magazine photographer. Author of several books; appeared in many exhibitions. Visited Israel frequently 1948-1956. Killed at Suez 1956, four days after armistice.

**Miriam Shamir**
Born Germany. Film-maker and photographer with especial interest in landscape and architecture. Wife of Israel's ambassador to Mali.

**Ann Zane Shanks**
Born United States. Magazine photographer, film-maker and writer. Author of several books; has appeared in many exhibitions. Visited Israel 1968. Lives in New York.

**Abraham Soskin**
Born Russia, emigrated to Israel 1905. Chronicled foundation and growth of Tel Aviv. One of founders of Israel Photographers' Union. Died 1963.

**Daniella Weihart**
Born Israel. Free-lance photographer. Lives in Tel Aviv.

**Yona Zaloscer**
Born Israel. Free-lance photographer. Lives in Haifa.

below / **Leonard Freed** / View from Shalom Building / Tel Aviv 1968
overleaf / Laying irrigation pipes in the fields / Hafez Hayyim 1968

above / Arab bride displaying her trousseau to village women / Majd el Qurum 1968

overleaf / Arab dancing at wedding party / Majd el Qurum 1968

**Leonard Freed** / Girls in Tel Aviv market / 1968

above / **Leonard Freed** / Moroccan on street in Beersheba

opposite / Cafe on Dizengoff Street / Tel Aviv 1968

overleaf / Machine shop, Dead Sea Works / Sedom 1968

Men die, heroically or fruitlessly, but man carries on. In Israel it is the same: the farmer must till the fields, the young must make love, and the photographer must, I suppose, be ready to photograph it all.

I know I am secretly honored to be photographing Israel in its love affair with life—life as it is lived in the hearts and minds of men. Working there is also like going home, in a land where the Prime Minister looks like my uncle Hyim, the Foreign Minister like uncle Benjamin, and the general of the army like cousin Lenny.

Everyone speaks of hope. Hope in Israel has a special meaning; for me, hope is to see the land, hope is to know the people, hope is to watch life go on.

—Leonard Freed

opposite / **Leonard Freed** / Shore near El Arish / 1967

below / **Micha Bar-Am** / Arab village elders offering coffee to Israeli soldiers / Samarian hills 1968

opposite / El Fatah commando in prison / 1968

Fatah commandos had crossed the Jordan and shelled a border kibbutz with a few mortar rounds. Starting back, they ran into an Israeli ambush. The leader was killed but the rest escaped in the dark. After searching the nearby hills and villages, we found six of the guerrillas in a cave. They smiled wearily, their hands raised, as if saying that as long as one was alive he could hope for a better future, even behind bars.

Is it human to give such a man a cigarette, knowing he would have shot you if he could? Is it human to put aside memories of friends killed? What is it makes you treat an enemy well, and even respect him?

I remember how the elders of a village being searched offered coffee to the soldiers. The tradition of hospitality is stronger than many an emotion in this country of strong, contradictory emotions. "Aren't we cousins," said an old sheik, "sons of Ishmael and Isaac?"

—Micha Bar-Am

below / **Micha Bar-Am** / Israeli patrol searching Arab village / Samarian hills 1968

opposite / Suspected guerrillas lined up for identification / Samarian hills 1968

overleaf / Israeli troops asking cooperation of Arab villagers / Samarian hills 1968

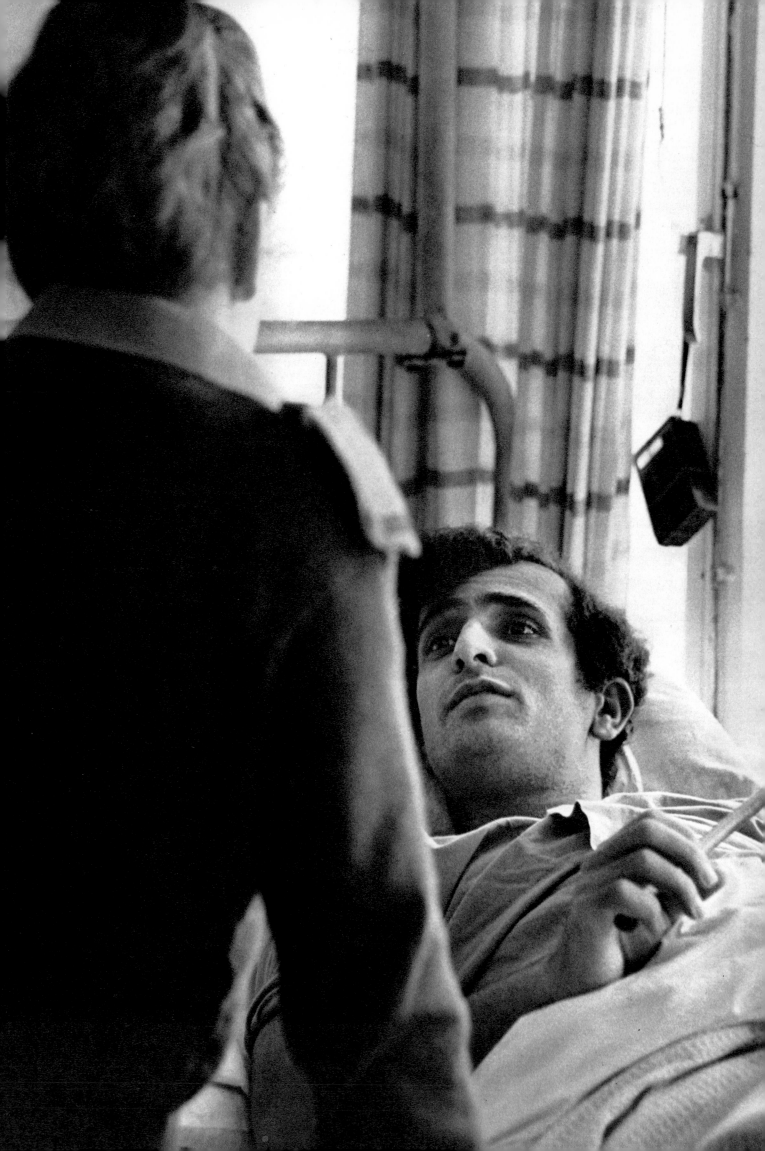

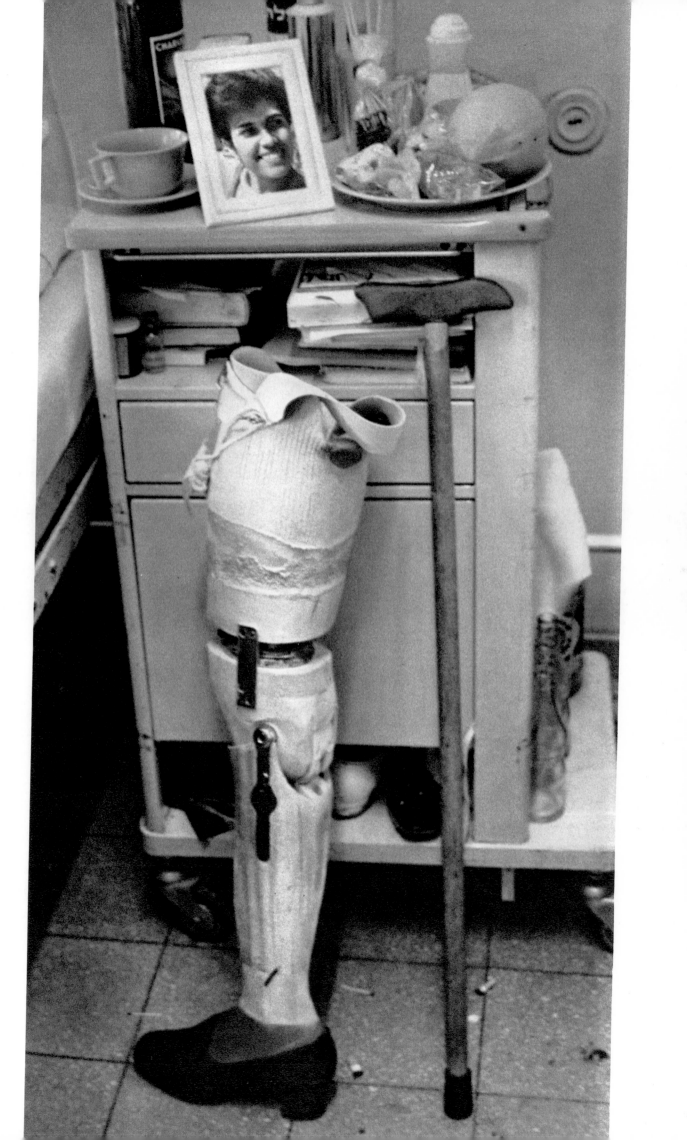

below / **Cornell Capa** / Lost Arab girl just returned from Jordan, asking help of Israeli policeman / Allenby Bridge August 1967

opposite / Food distribution center at UNRWA camp / Nablus August 1967

overleaf / **Yona Zaloscer** / Rehabilitation center, Tel-Hashomer Hospital / Near Tel Aviv 1969

below / **Cornell Capa** / Arab cursing in ruins of home / Qalqiliya August 1967

opposite / Egyptian soldiers awaiting repatriation / Near Suez Canal June 1967

below / **Micha Bar-Am** / Chief military rabbi Shlomo Goren at the Western Wall / Jerusalem June 7, 1967
opposite / **David Rubinger** / Paratroopers at the Western Wall / Jerusalem June 7, 1967
overleaf / **Leonard Freed** / Mea Shearim resident passing gutted tanks / Jerusalem June 1967

The entire nation was exalted, and many wept, when they heard of the capture of the Old City. Our sabra youth, and most certainly our soldiers, do not tend to be sentimental, and they shrink from any public show of feeling. But the strain of battle, the anxiety which preceded it, and the sense of salvation and of direct confrontation with Jewish history itself, cracked the shell of hardness and shyness and released wellsprings of emotion and stirrings of the spirit. The paratroopers who conquered the Western Wall leaned on its stones and wept....

A strange phenomenon can be observed among our soldiers. Their joy is incomplete, and their celebration is marred by sorrow and shock. There are even some who abstain from celebration entirely. The men in the front lines saw with their own eyes not only the glory of victory, but also the price of victory—their comrades fallen beside them soaked in blood. I know that the terrible price paid by our enemies also touched the hearts of many of our men. It may be that the Jewish people has never learned and has never accustomed itself to the triumph of conquest and victory, with the result that we accept them with mixed feelings.

—Major General Yitzhak Rabin, from an address delivered in the ceremony at which the Hebrew University of Jerusalem conferred upon him an honorary doctorate of philosophy, June 28, 1967

opposite / **Charles Harbutt** / Samaritan Chief Rabbi Amram Ben-Yitzhak Hacohen at Passover services / Mount Gerizim 1967

overleaf / **Cornell Capa** / Soldiers praying at dawn, while Egyptian planes approach / Sinai June 6, 1967

In the fall of 1966, I went to the Holy Land, as had so many thousands before me, as a pilgrim. My concern was to photograph the rituals and places of Palestine evoking the Jewish pastoral milieu in which Christ was reared, and to attend and record Christian festivals. As is inevitable in the Holy Land, since Christmas falls close to Ramadan and Easter to Passover, I also witnessed major Moslem and Jewish festivals, passing back and forth between Israel and Jordan. And, as is also tragically true in the Holy Land, Christmastime was filled with talk of a commando raid, Easter with memories of an air battle over Galilee and evidence of growing mobilization in Jordan, all finally capped by the Six Day War.

While real estate, far more than religion, has been the cause of war in Palestine from biblical days, still the fervor of religion misapplied, until it divides mankind rather than unites it, is to be held deeply guilty. Today religious tensions and hatreds persist, obstructing rational solution and generating sorrow after sorrow. This one pilgrim found the holiest of holies slowly change, for him, into an ugliest of uglies.

—Charles Harbutt

opposite / **Charles Harbutt** / Lebanese pilgrims on the Via Dolorosa, Good Friday / Jerusalem 1967
overleaf / Orthodox Feast of the Holy Fire in the aedicule of the Church of the Holy Sepulcher, Easter Saturday / Jerusalem 1967

above / **Paul Schutzer** / Orthodox class / Jerusalem 1960

opposite / Girl air force officer / 1960

Soldier in training / The Negev 1965

**Paul Schutzer** / Four-day march from Tel Aviv to Jerusalem / 1965

I am free to tear up my American roots and live in Israel. I would do well there—we would all flourish and grow. But for me, Israel is a spiritual thing: not a place to live but an inspiration on how to live.

—Paul Schutzer, from a letter to his daughter, April 1, 1965

To ask you not to worry is silly. What more can I say than I'm in Israel, and you know this is where I want to be.

—From his last letter to his wife before his death in the Sinai battle, June 5, 1967

below / **Paul Schutzer** / Moroccan Jew kissing rabbi's beard as sign of respect / 1960

opposite / Kurd mother nursing child / Near Jerusalem 1960

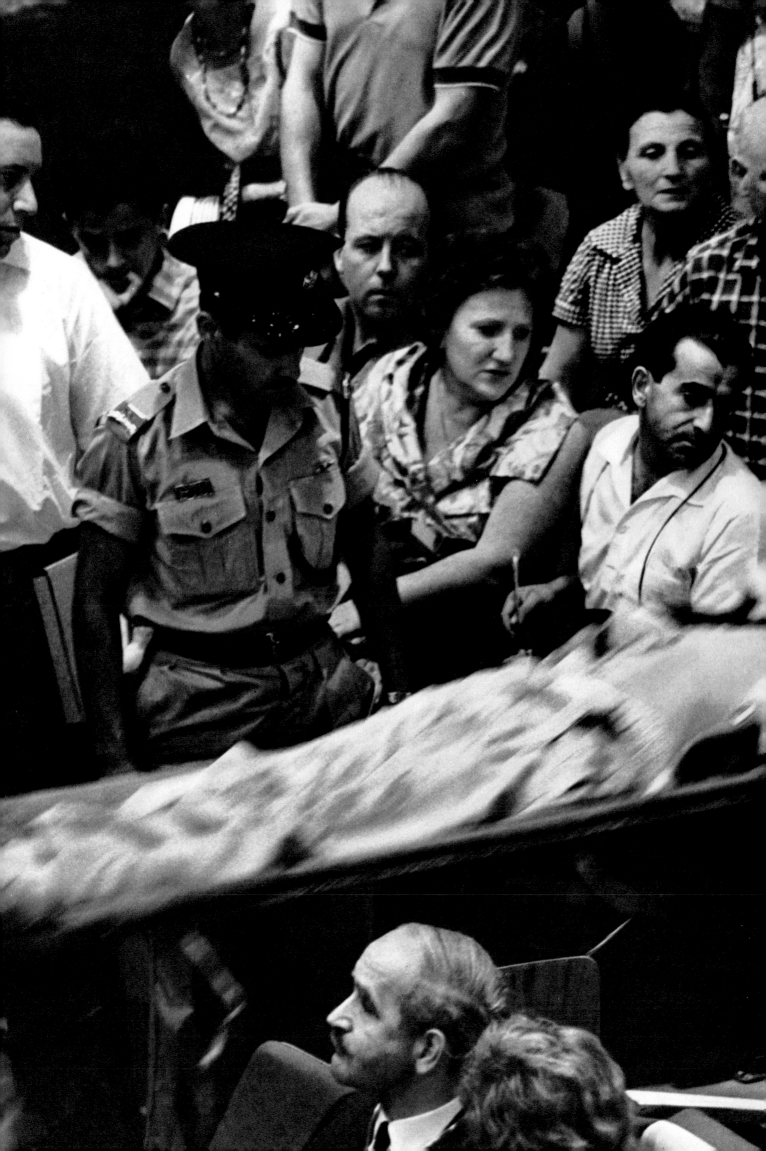

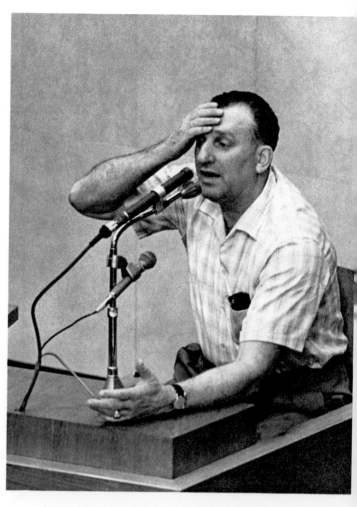

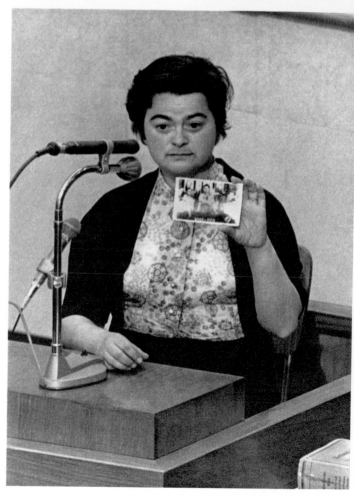

Adolf Eichmann will enjoy a privilege he did not accord to even a one of his victims. He will be able to defend himself before the court. His fate will be decided according to the law and the evidence, with the burden of proof resting on the prosecution.

And the judges of Israel will pronounce true and righteous judgment.

—Gideon Hausner, from his opening statement


I was in the iron grip of orders.

Legally I am innocent.

—Adolf Eichmann


The dispatch by the accused of every train carrying a thousand souls to Auschwitz or to any of the other places of extermination amounted to direct participation by the accused in one thousand acts of premeditated murder, and his legal and moral responsibility for those murders is in no way less than the measure of liability of him who put those persons with his own hands into the gas chambers.

—From the sentence

opposite / **Israel Government Press Office** / Adolf Eichmann testifying / Jerusalem 1961

I started this set of photographs on the Carmel market more or less by chance. It took me a couple of months, and I came again and again to shoot. It is the only subject I have covered so fully, and that I have felt such compulsion to do. I had a strange feeling that, for the first time in my life, I could with one shot know a person very well. Maybe that opinion is mistaken, but later in looking at these photographs I felt that I had known these people for a long time.

Then there came one day when I decided I had done it. What I could do, I had done. The set was finished; it was a complete circle, a gift of destiny. I could then only repeat myself, and weaken its impact.

—Paul Gross

below and next five pages / **Paul Gross** / Carmel market / Tel Aviv 1962-1963

The festival takes place in May in the town of Merón, on the anniversary of the death of Rabbi Simon Bar-Yochai, whose tomb is the center of the festival. He was a spiritual leader of the Jews during the first century, and led them in a revolt against the Romans. Every year Orthodox Jews make a pilgrimage to the tomb, where they believe they will insure good luck for the year. The holiday lasts from evening through the following afternoon. During the night people camp out and bonfires are lit. Wishes are made by throwing special candles into the bonfires. In the morning, the chief rabbi cuts the forelocks of three-year-old boys as a sign that they are no longer babies. They sit on their fathers' shoulders, and the fathers dance around in the courtyard of the tomb. The little boys cry and the fathers are very proud.

The festival has no name.

—Ken Heyman

below and next five pages / **Ken Heyman** / Festival at Merón / 1965

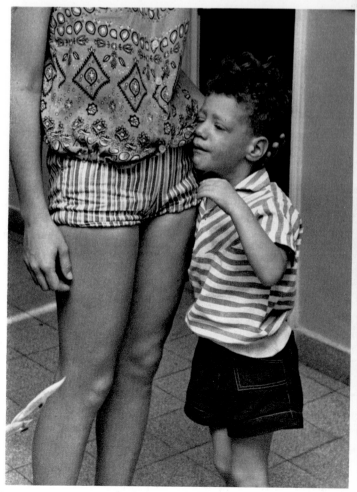

After my military service I spent a year in a young kibbutz in the Negev, where there were ten children whom I grew attached to, and who were perfect subjects for my photographs. Later I returned to the kibbutz to start a family, and now I have a son of my own. I have portrayed him and his group of friends from the beginning of their lives.

Many ask me how I photograph children naturally. This is an open secret: you cannot photograph naturally, especially not children, if you seem a foreign body to them, if they do not know and are not used to you, if they fear the instrument—the camera—in your hands. I enter the group, spend many hours with them, play with them, talk, tell tales, and become one of the group. They become used to me, have faith in me, and act in my presence with utmost freedom.

—Moshe Lapidot

below and next three pages / **Moshe Lapidot** / Children's house at Mizra / 1968

above / **Shlomo Arad** / Army radio operator / Sinai 1969

below / **Peter Fink** / Technician, Weizmann Institute / Rehovot 1967

above / **Boris Carmi** / Habani silversmith / Near Lod 1959

below / **Peter Merom** / Kibbutz couple / Hulata 1965

opposite / **Simpson Kalisher** / Elder teaching in synagogue / 1962

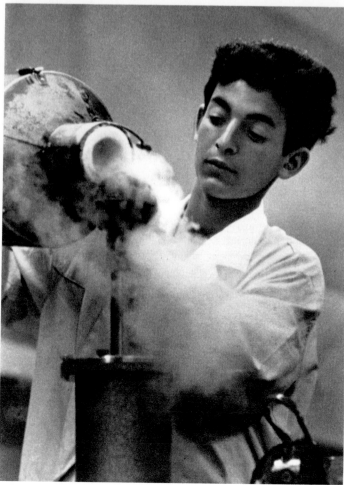

above / **Mordo Abramov** / Young girl / Kibbutz Yakum about 1960

below / **Gideon Raz** / Old man

above / **Yitzhak Ostrovsky** / Old man / 1966

below / **Ann Zane Shanks** / Arab girl / Golan Heights, 1968

above / **Gideon Raz** / Paratrooper / 1967
below / **Erich Hartmann** / Housewife / Ramat David 1958

above / **Erich Hartmann** / Young man / Eilat 1958
below / **Boris Carmi** / Bedouin woman / Paran Valley 1968

opposite / **David Perlmutter** / Girl soldier / about 1968
above / **Simpson Kalisher** / Grape farmer / Jerusalem 1962
below / **David Seymour** / Moroccan farm worker / 1953

above / **Erich Hartmann** / Mime / Tel Aviv 1957
below / **Daniella Weihart** / Levana Finkelstein / 1968

above / **Rolf Kneller** / S. Y. Agnon / about 1964-1965

below / **Rolf Kneller** / Yitzhak Pugacz / 1965

above / **David Harris** / Yohanan Aharoni / 1961

below / **Rolf Kneller** / Avraham Goldberg / 1964

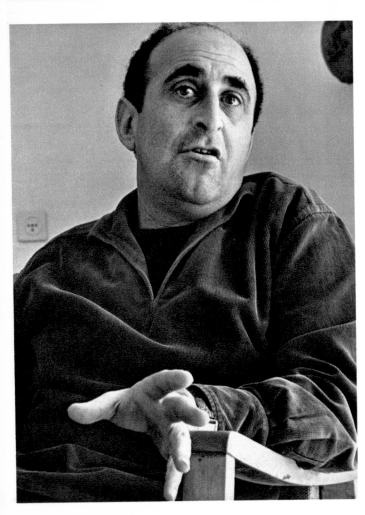

above / **Rolf Kneller** / Martin Buber / 1958

below / **Rolf Kneller** / Mordechai Levanon / 1964

above / **David Maestro** / Aharon Ashkenazi / 1966

below / **Mordo Avrahamov** / Avraham Shlonski / 1966

above / **Efrem Ilani** / Pinhas Litvinovsky / 1967

below / **David Harris** / James Biberkraut and Yigael Yadin / 1961

above / **Rolf Kneller** / Moshe Dayan / 1968

below / **Peter Fink** / Meyer Weisgal / 1966

In 1952, I was in bed one day with a high fever when the editor of *Paris-Match* called, asking me to leave immediately for Israel. That same evening, I stuffed myself with pills and took the plane—how could I have refused a trip of which I had dreamed since childhood?

Once my news assignment was finished, I travelled through the country with my camera, for my own pleasure and without preconceived plans. I sought only to fill my eyes with the spectacle of this land, which I recognized as if I had lived here before: the landscapes of Judea and the Negev, the ramparts of Jerusalem, the shepherds of Galilee. Near Beersheba I met Ruth in the fields. I saw Anne Frank and her companions planting trees in the Judean hills.

At the end of my visit, leafing through my prints, I knew that I had seen only what I was looking for: the land of the Bible, and the memories of my childhood. To see the other face of Israel, that of the new state, would be a very different task. One day I will surely undertake it.

—Izis (Israel Bidermanas)

above / **Izis** / Bedouin children / Near Beersheba 1952

below / Road worker / Between Beersheba and Sedom 1952

above / Kibbutz shepherd / Daphne 1952

below / Old man at planting of memorial trees / Near Jerusalem 1952

below / Yemenite family / 1952

overleaf / Cobbler / Tel Aviv 1952

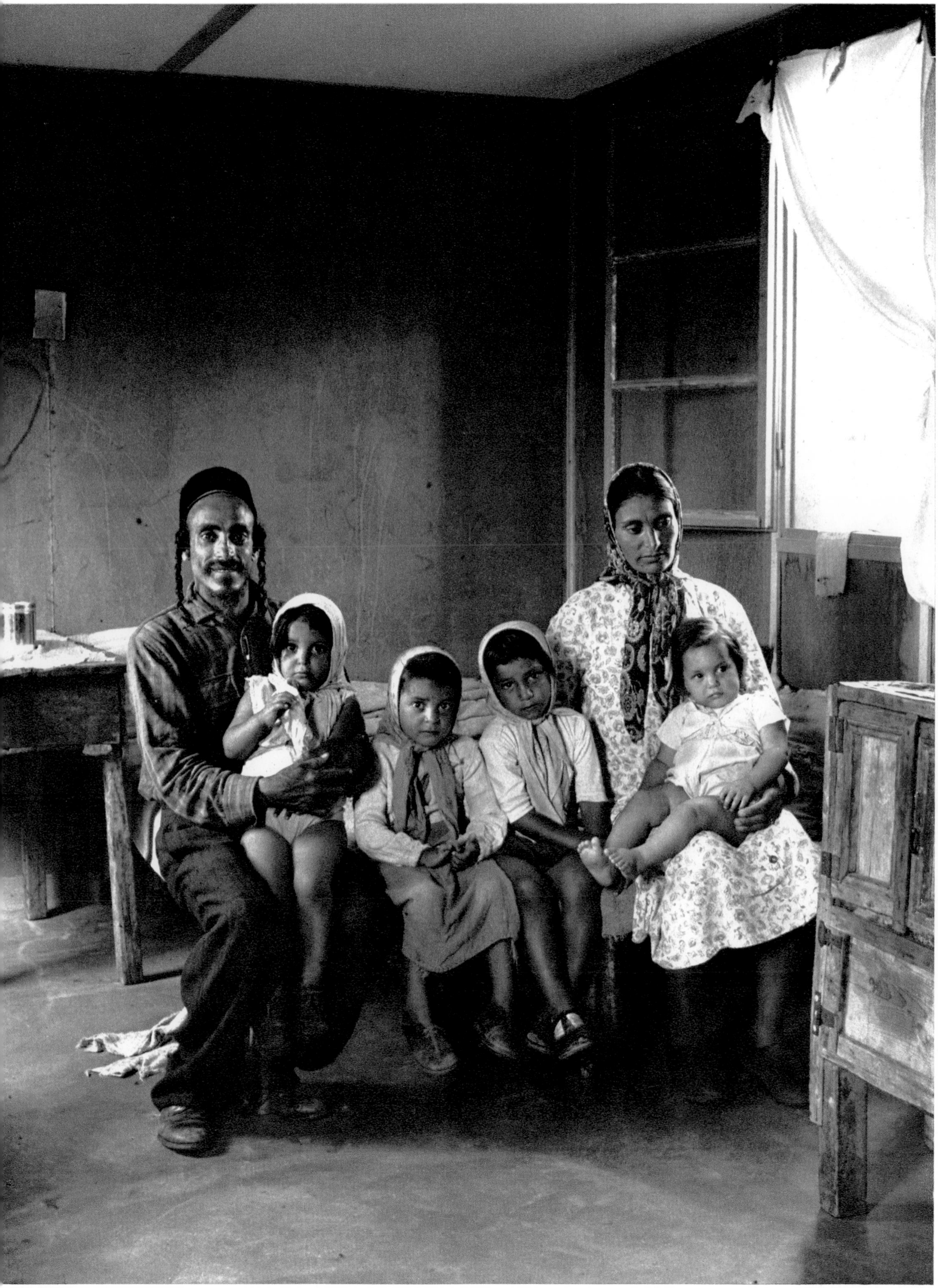

It was like coming home again. It was like picking up the living threads of my life, for which I had been searching in vain on the heaps of rubble and ash in the ruins of Warsaw.

—David Seymour ("Chim"), from a letter to his sister, 1948

Chim picked up his camera the way a doctor takes his stethoscope out of his bag, applying his diagnosis to the condition of the heart. His own was vulnerable.

—Henri Cartier-Bresson, on the tenth anniversary of David Seymour's death, November 10, 1956, by Egyptian gunfire

below / **David Seymour** / Kibbutz wedding / 1953

opposite / Kibbutz farmer / 1948

**David Seymour** / First child born in Alma, settlement of Italian immigrants / 1951

You get close to what you photograph here. Close to the tattered people coming off the immigrant boats in Haifa. And to those in the tent cities during the huge immigration wave of the early fifties. Or to the guy who feverishly hacks away at the sand in the Negev and really believes that it will be green tomorrow.

You also knew the fellow lying in a pool of his own blood in the border settlement near Hebron. And you know the aunt of the one you photographed with his throat slit by Fedayeen raiders, because she lives next door to you.

Identification—the magic word of the magazine photographers—that is one thing that comes easy here.

—David Rubinger

below / **David Rubinger** / David Ben Gurion, Golda Meir, and Joseph Burg (Minister of Social Welfare) in the Knesset / 1955

opposite / First oil strike in the Negev / Heletz 1955

below / **David Rubinger** / Yemenite farmer / Near Beersheba 1956
opposite / Victim of Jordanian machine-gunner across truce line / Ramat Rachel, Jerusalem 1956
overleaf / Military funeral / Mount Herzl, Jerusalem 1957

Zion, many lands are beautiful,
But no eye has seen the equal of thy beauty.
I know not whether the skies bow to thee,
Or whether thou ascendest to the skies.
—Judah al-Harizi, twelfth century

below / **Peter Merom** / Mountains in the southern Negev / 1961

opposite / **Amiram Erev** / Door, Monastery of St. Catherine / Sinai 1968

below / **Boris Carmi** / Rock formation / Sinai 1967

opposite / **Archie Lieberman** / Cave near Sedom / 1960

above / **Amiram Erev** / Wadi Mukkateb / Sinai 1968

below / **Miriam Shamir** / Mountain in southern Negev

**Rolf Kneller** / Israel Museum / Jerusalem 1964

When we were young, we loved to wander barefoot along its shores, through the damp weeds, across the slick mudflats of our small lake—Lake Huleh in Galilee. We saw the lake as part of the First Creation, and we pledged ourselves to it unconditionally, loving it in its placid moments, in its stormy hours, always. Boats and fish and nets and oars were magic words. Our dory pierced the veil concealing that marvelous feathered world of the lake fowl. Our oars penetrated the secrets of the cane, the sedge, the reeds.

Years passed like this. We knew about the plans to turn the lake into dry land, to bury the swamp-borne malaria in the dried-out clods of the recovered soil. But nothing changed. It seemed as though things would always be the same.

But one day the die was cast. Suddenly a giant dredging machine gleamed in the sunlight. The steel monster broke through the swamp and cut into the lake itself. The condemned lake died and rotted before our eyes. The earth, cracked and split with drying, cried out as the millions of lake creatures perished, open-mouthed and gasping. The proud greenery mourned and withered.

After a time—even with startling quickness—sugarcane and cotton sprang up in the fields which had once been hunting grounds for fishermen, as though they had grown there since the beginning of the world. And we will stroll in the new fields, we will celebrate the holiday of the plowed earth, but in our heart is a memory and an echo . . .

And our thankfulness to the lake for the days of our youth.

—Peter Merom, from *The Death of the Lake*

next seven pages / **Peter Merom** / The death of Lake Huleh / Hulata 1959

The only thing I ever envied the angels was their wings. And if there were any truth in the transmigration of souls, I always hoped mine might be sneaked into an eagle's egg.

My profession finally became my Jacob's ladder into the sky. I simply decided one day to give myself an assignment to shoot aerial photographs in the Negev. Many flying hours followed, and soon, very fortunately, I didn't have to give myself the assignment any more. But to tell the truth, the factories, hotels, or settlements I am asked to photograph simply provide me an excuse to have another look at our little country from above.

It is the unusual pattern, unseen from the ground, that I look for. One such is the Kennedy memorial at Jerusalem. The road leading to it goes spiraling around the hill, and when I went there sightseeing I began to imagine what a view it must make from above. On my next assignment to Jerusalem, I asked the pilot to make a little detour to the monument; I was not disappointed. Another example is the Herodion near Bethlehem. From the ground one sees only a bare hill, which must be climbed to reveal the ruins of Herod's palace. But from the air one beholds the whole surreal construction.

I prefer to shoot from a small Piper. First you circle the subject, searching for the right angle; then, having gained altitude, you glide sideways down to the danger point, the motor almost shut off, shooting away as fast as you can. One downswoop is rarely enough, so up you go in the tightest possible turn, and glide down again and again. The pilot has to do everything with very little explanation, because it is hard to hear above the roar of the engine and the whine of the wind through the open door. Yes, the door has to be open, since you cannot shoot sharp pictures through plexiglass.

—Werner Braun

opposite / **Werner Braun** / Nabi Moussa shrine / Near Jericho 1968

overleaf, left / Ruins of the Herodion / Near Bethlehem 1968

overleaf, right / John F. Kennedy Memorial and Forest / Near Jerusalem 1966

I love the skyline of the desert. Its mountains make the deepest impression upon me of all the creations of God; there is a tangible, primeval power within the rocks. I also love the skyline of skyscrapers, but I still do not know whether we have succeeded in building the land without making it ugly. There might have been an alternative to building thousands of cubelike housing projects; our buildings could perhaps blend into the landscape as well as the Arab buildings do, as if they had been built by nature itself.

When I am afraid I am taking a commonplace, cluttered picture, I try, in different ways, to come closer to my subject—to fall upon it. But since I am not interested in photographing single details, I often choose, as a solution, the panorama.

Only rarely, when I look about me, do I feel that the world is beautiful.

—Amiram Erev

below / **Amiram Erev** / Sections of aqueduct pipe / Near Ashkelon 1959

opposite / Steelworker, pipe plant / Near Acre 1953

overleaf, above / View from Mount Moses / Sinai 1968

overleaf, below / Institute of Technology / Haifa 1966

preceding overleaf, above / **Amiram Erev** / Couple on Mediterranean cruise / 1968

preceding overleaf, below / Nahal unit on "Snake Path" to Masada / 1949

below / Textile mill and workers' housing, Mount Tabor in distance / Nazareth 1960

opposite / Banquet celebrating contract signing for construction of port of Ashdod / 1961

Jerusalem is built out of the limestone of the Judaean hills, and every stone comes to life once the sunshine touches it, giving the city as a whole a strangely luminous quality all its own.

No one is a stranger in Jerusalem. All of us have, since childhood, carried in our hearts some image of this most universal of cities. And yet, since no one is a stranger here, who can find words with equal meaning for all? Jerusalem is far too personal: everyone must come and sing his own song.

—Richard Cleave

above / **Richard Cleave** / Dome of the Rock / Jerusalem 1968

overleaf / Interior, Dome of the Rock / Jerusalem 1968

Bring us in peace from the four corners of the earth, and lead us upright to our land.

Recall our dispersed from among the nations, and gather our scattered people from the ends of the earth.

—From the Prayer Book

Israel is the crudest and hardest place one can live today. It is also a place where one hears the young sing at night, and even the old ones talk about the future.

The ships carrying the immigrants are newly bought boats, in reality broken-down steamers with a long history of running the British blockade, or small schooners bringing in Jews from the ghettos of surrounding Moslem countries. The immigrants on these boats are the motley remains of a people who two thousand years ago left these shores to scatter to the far corners of the earth and are now coming back, most of them to live and some of them to die, in the Holy Land.

Curiously, the present state owes its existence just as much to Hitler and Bevin as to its own accomplishments. Without Nazism it could never have gotten mass immigration, and without Bevin to encourage the Arabs to fight and flee, it would never have gotten its present territory. But the new country, born out of victorious battle, is granted no peace.

—Robert Capa, 1948

opposite / **Robert Capa** / Farmer building new settlement / 1949

overleaf / Immigrants / Haifa 1948

above / **Boris Carmi** / Palmach unit during War of Liberation / Ben Shemen 1948

opposite / Soldier throwing grenade / Between Tel Aviv and Jaffa 1948

overleaf / Cavalry unit on patrol / near Tel Aviv 1948

**Werner Braun** / British demolition in retaliation against Jewish underground attacks / Ben Yehuda Street, Jerusalem 1947

We Jews understand and deeply sympathize with the urge of the Arab people for unity, independence, and progress, and our Arab neighbors, I hope, will realize that the Jews in their historic homeland can, under no conditions, be made to remain a subordinate, dependent minority as they are in all other countries in the Diaspora. The Jewish nation in its own country must become a free and independent state.

—David Ben-Gurion, 1947

below and opposite / **United Israel Appeal Photo Archives** / Illegal immigrants being deported / Haifa 1947

above / **Yaakov Ben-Dov** / Boating party of Jerusalem students / Jordan River near Jericho 1912

below / **Zvi Oron** / British High Commissioner's garden party on the King's birthday / Jerusalem 1934

overleaf / **Yaakov Ben-Dov** / Volunteers of Jewish Legion, serving in the British Army against the Turks / El Arish 1918

above / **Yaakov Ben-Dov** / Drawing water from the Jordan / Near Degania 1911 or 1912

below / Shepherdesses from a new settlement / Jezreel Valley early 1920s

A state cannot be created by decree but only by the forces of the people and in the course of generations. Even if all the governments of the world gave us a country, it would be a gift of words. But if the Jewish people will go and build Palestine, the Jewish State will become a reality and a fact.

—Chaim Weizmann, commenting on the Balfour Declaration, 1917

**Abraham Soskin** / Founders of Tel Aviv casting lots for building sites / 1909

Children exercising in schoolyard / Jerusalem 1911

**Leo Kann** / Yemenite silversmiths, Bezalel Art Center / Jerusalem 1911

Watchman in Judean settlement / 1911

As I had heard the most contradictory descriptions of the Holy Land, and the most divergent reports on the effectiveness of its colonization—I was still a student with little time and less money—I decided to finish my studies and then go to Palestine. Then I was asked to make this journey, which originally would have satisfied only my own selfish wishes, as a service to the Jewish people: to take systematic and comprehensive pictures of Palestine, as effective demonstration of Herzl's holy ideas, and testimonial proof of the rebirth of our ancestors' homeland. I now want to give my work to the public. May it give to the faithful among my people fulfillment of their hope, and may it show to the timid and doubtful how proud and strong stands the ancient Jewish trunk on holy ground, and how freshly and wonderfully it blossoms.

—Leo Kann, 1912

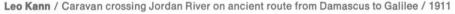

**Leo Kann** / Caravan crossing Jordan River on ancient route from Damascus to Galilee / 1911